THE HEYDAY OF LEEDS HOLBECK AND ITS LOCOMOTIVES

Gavin Morrison

Above:
It was appropriate that the rebuilt Royal Scot No 46145 *The Duke of Wellington's Regt (West Riding)* should be allocated to Holbeck Depot. Prior to its allocation, in around January 1953, it had been shedded at Holyhead and Longsight. I observed the locomotive having a major overhaul at Crewe Works in February 1959, which was probably its last until it finally left Holbeck in October 1961, on transfer to Low Moor. In fact it went to Farnley Junction for storage, where it remained until 23 September 1963 when it was steamed again and hauled Nos 46130 and 46103 to Crewe works, where they were scrapped.

All photos by Gavin Morrison unless shown otherwise.

First published 1994

ISBN 0 7110 2225 9

Designed by Ian Allan Studio

Published by Ian Allan Publishing an imprint of Ian Allan Ltd, Terminal House, Station Approach, Shepperton, Surrey TW17 8AS; and printed by Ian Allan Printing Ltd, Coombelands House, Coombelands Lane, Addlestone Weybridge, Surrey KT15 1HY.

Introduction

Whilst compiling this album under the title of the 'Heyday of Leeds Holbeck and its Locomotives,' I am aware that what I consider the heyday may well be at variance with other enthusiasts. There can be few enthusiasts around today who remember the depot being full of immaculate red locomotives, whilst there will be many who possibly feel the heyday was when Holbeck had an allocation of around 40 'Peaks' in the 1970s. For me the period from 1957 to the end of the steam on 30 September 1967 was the heyday of Holbeck, when I knew the staff and locomotives well, and so it is on this 10-year period that this book is concentrated.

The detailed history has been well documented in other publications such as *LMS Engine Sheds*, Wild Swan Publications, but a few historical facts will not go amiss.

It was opened on 8 May 1868, so last year celebrated its 125 years of active service, but the event passed almost unnoticed.

There were two main sheds which were square constructions with a turntable inside, giving in fact two roundhouses. In addition there was an eight-road repair depot. The original turntable in No 1 shed was 42ft, but this was increased in size to 55ft in 1902 and then to 60ft in 1938 which was large enough for most locomotives allocated. The exception was the Gresley 'A3s' which had a brief spell at Holbeck between 1960 and 1962, these locomotives used to have to turn on Whitehall triangle.

Under the Midland Railway coding Holbeck was allocated No 28 and had an allocation of about 50 locomotives when opened. A sub-depot at Stourton was built in 1893 mainly for freight and shunting locomotives, whilst Holbeck looked after the passenger fleet.

Holbeck depot apparently employed about 700 people at one time, possibly in the 1930s, as in 1934 it had an allocation of 109, with 63 at the sub-shed at Stourton. By this time the depot had been recoded 20A by the LMS.

The early classes allocated were mainly the Midland 2-2-2s, 2-4-0s and Kirtley 0-6-0s, but by the turn of the century the various Midland 4-4-0s dominated the express passenger work with 0-6-0s for the freight, and it was not until 1960 that the last two 4-4-0s left the allocation.

In 1930 there were 12 'Claughtons' on the books for working north, and south to Leicester. However, these were gradually replaced by new 'Patriots' and by 1933 there were only five 'Claughtons' remaining with seven new 'Patriots'. Three of these remained until 1943, but the arrival of the rebuilt 'Scots' finally saw their departure. There was of course during this period a build-up of 'Jubilees' and Stanier Class 5s.

The depot is probably best remembered for its association with the rebuilt 'Scots', some of them remaining at the depot for around 18 years, until being succeeded by the Class 45 'Peaks'. It should also be mentioned that some 'Jubilees' had around 25 years of continuous allocation to the depot. No doubt the same could be said for many Midland Compounds.

Many improvements were carried out over the years, the major ones being the construction of a 300 ton capacity coaler in 1935 together with an ash plant, plus roof repairs in 1937 and 1942. Another major installation in 1956 was an electrically driven turntable in No 1 Shed, which was much appreciated by the staff.

The depot was responsible for working many famous trains over the years eg: the 'Devonian,' the 'Waverley,' the 'Thames-Forth,' but the 'Thames Clyde' express is undoubtedly the most famous.

In 1957 the Leeds area became part of the North Eastern Region, and the depot was allocated the code 55A. This had little effect on the type of locomotives based at the shed, but in 1960 some Gresley 'A3' Pacifics were drafted in to work the Scottish Express. This was a surprise move, particularly as diesels were already appearing, but proved short lived as by 1962 the Class 45 'Peaks' had taken over and the 'A3s' returned to the northeast from whence they had come. It must be said the Holbeck crews had some affection for the 'A3s' and enjoyed the comfortable cabs and free steaming boilers.

As the diesels took over more and more details in the area, other steam depots such as Copley Hill, Farnley Junction and Stourton were closed and their duties and staff concentrated at Holbeck. This resulted in Holbeck men, who already had a wide route knowledge, being passed for even more destinations, which in 1966 included Bristol, Nottingham, St Pancras, Barrow in Furness, Glasgow, Kings Cross and Liverpool, to name but a few.

The relentless progress of dieselisation eventually caught up with Holbeck when on 30 September 1967 it closed to steam, although the last steam locomotive, which was Class 5 No 45428,

Front cover:
The most famous train worked by Holbeck Depot was the 'Thames-Clyde Express'. The rebuilt 'Royal Scots' provided the motive power on most occasions between 1943 and 1960. No 46145 *The Duke of Wellington's Regt (West Riding)* is shown ready to leave Leeds City station on 28 February 1960.

didn't leave until August 1968, when it departed for Tyseley. The shed buildings, together with the massive coaling plant were demolished in 1970 and the site rebuilt as a diesel maintenance depot. By 1973 it was the largest locomotive diesel depot in the West Riding with an allocation of 79.

With the introduction of the HSTs on the Inter City workings from May 1979, Holbeck crews were re-trained for 125mph running and the new techniques this involved. The introduction of the HSTs, which were serviced at Neville Hill Depot, resulted in Holbeck being discontinued as a diesel maintenance depot, except for minor repairs and fuelling.

After the sectorisation of British Rail, Holbeck became a sub-depot to Tinsley under Railfreight Distribution. In April 1992 Railfreight Distribution pulled out leaving only the Parcels Sector and Civil Engineers using the site. It was inevitable that the depot would not last, and so when the Parcels Sector decided it could make alternative arrangements for the stabling of its locomotives when in Leeds, it was decided that the site should close as a fuelling and stabling point as from 4 October 1993. I have listed the locomotives which were present on the last morning, Class 37, No 37045 being the very last to be fuelled. Fuelling facilities will be retained on the site, but will only be used in the case of emergencies.

I hope that some of the staff from the 1960s will still be around to see this album, and that it may bring back memories to them. Many of the photographs would not have been possible without the assistance of Shed Master Tom Geeson, District Motive Power Superintendent Tom Greavens, Inspectors Albert Pullan and Geoff Wilson, the many Scottish Link Drivers who welcomed me into the cab for official and unofficial footplate rides to Carlisle and Glasgow, and in later years Supervisors Brian Wilds and Martin Batson. To all of them I owe a great debt, and dedicate this album to them.

Right:
No collection of photographs about Holbeck Depot could be complete without including one of the famous Midland 'Compounds', which were allocated to the depot for over 50 years. The last compounds to be allocated to Holbeck were Nos 41100 and 41063 which were still active in April 1958 when they double headed an Ian Allan special between Leeds and Crewe via Standedge. Unfortunately I have not been able to locate a good colour slide of one of the class on the depot, so I have included this picture of Lancaster-allocated No 40931 taken on 17 August 1958. Records show that in 1920 Holbeck had an allocation of 13 compounds and in 1945 it still had eight.

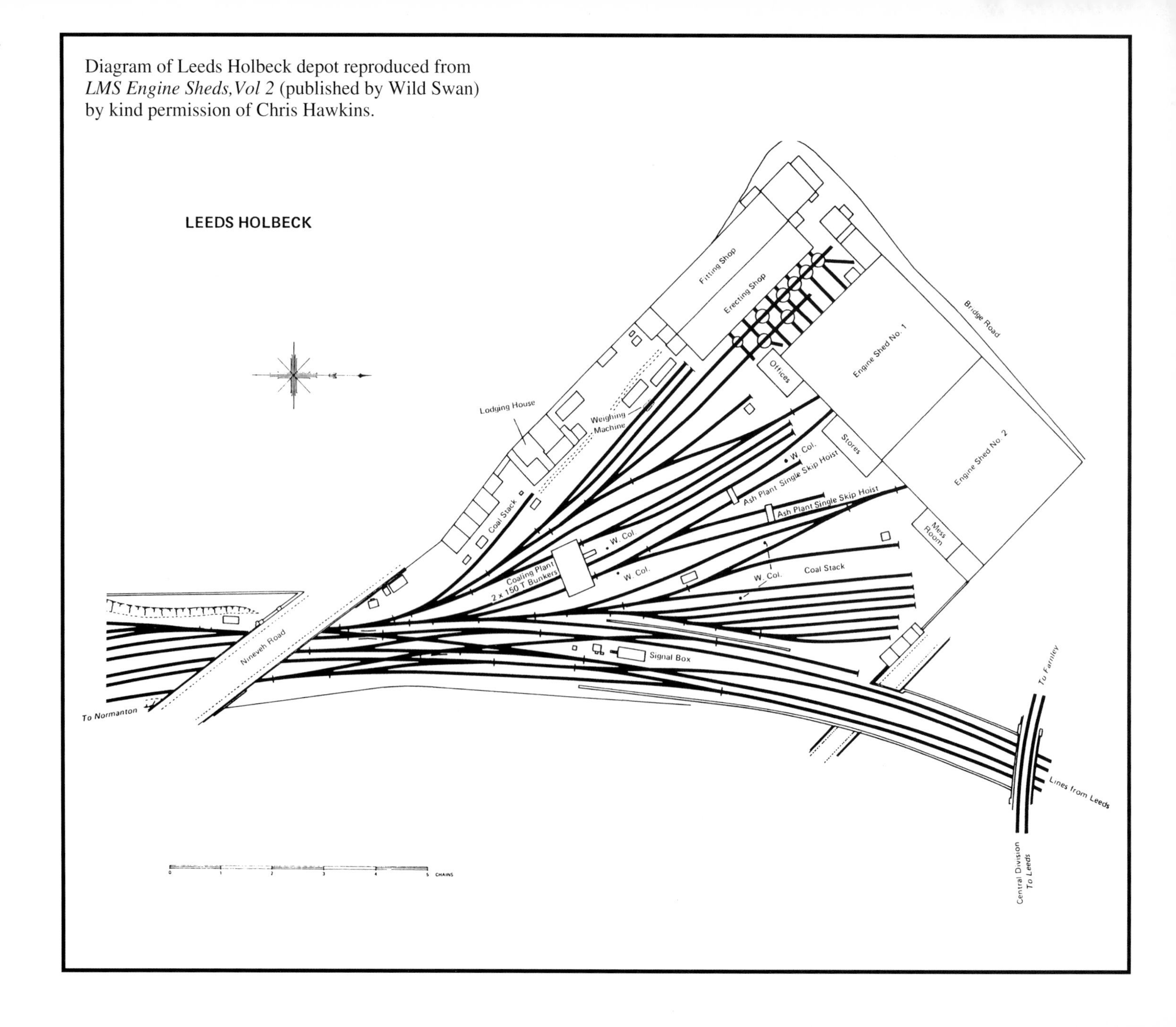

Diagram of Leeds Holbeck depot reproduced from *LMS Engine Sheds, Vol 2* (published by Wild Swan) by kind permission of Chris Hawkins.

Above:
When this picture was taken on 8 November 1967, the depot had been closed to steam since the 30 September. Looking immaculate, but with nowhere to go, one of the depot's best known Class 5s No 45428 awaits its move into preservation.

The locomotive had been allocated to the depot in December 1955 and, no doubt, the main event in its career was when it was selected as stand-by locomotive for the Royal Train working to Ripon on 30 May 1967. The locomotive which hauled the train was 'Jubilee' No 45562 *Alberta* which is seen in the background.
I believe the shed staff who repainted the locomotive for the occasion in plain black, actually painted the boiler bands in red, but the district motive power superintendent ordered them to be removed.

Left:
A view looking through the coaler at the depot on 20 October 1963 sees 'B1' No 61249 approaching to have its tender filled. By this date the locomotive had lost its name of *Fitzherbert Wright* and was probably allocated to York Depot. Built by North British Locomotive Co in October 1947, it lasted until June 1964. In the 1960s 'B1s' were frequent visitors to the depot. The hugh coaler had a capacity of 300 tons and was demolished with explosives in 1970.

Right:
The rebuilt 'Royal Scots' continued to be regular visitors to the depot after its own allocation left in 1961. Many of the class finished their working days allocated to Carlisle Kingmoor Depot working freights and local services over the Settle-Carlisle line to Leeds. No 46128 minus *The Lovat Scouts* nameplates, and in terrible external condition, visited the depot on 18 October 1963. It was withdrawn in October 1965. Also present on this date was Class 5 No 44810, a Saltley-based locomotive for many years.

46128
44810
44810

45562
55A

Left:
Shown in its customary immaculate condition during the locomotive's last year of service, the best known of the Holbeck 'Jubilees', and the last to be withdrawn, No 45562 *Alberta* rests inside the depot on Sunday 20 August 1967, no doubt having worked over the Settle-Carlisle on the Saturday. The locomotive is recorded as being allocated to the depot back in 1945, as were 12 other members of the class which were still at Holbeck at the time of withdrawal. It would appear that No 45562 and others may have had at least 25 years' continuous allocation to the Holbeck district.

Above:
After 17 years of working the Scottish express north from Leeds, assisted by 'Jubilees' and 'Britannias', the reign of the rebuilt 'Scots' came to an unexpected end with the arrival of redundant 'A3s' from the northeast in March 1960.

The condition of most of these locomotives was not exactly ex-works, and as Neville Hill Depot still had its allocation of 'A3s' with little work for them, Holbeck used to 'borrow' them as they were in better condition.

A Neville Hill locomotive for many years, No 60084 *Trigo* glistens in the evening sun. It is probably being prepared for one of the sleeper expresses on 17 March 1961.

Below:
The sight of one of Polmadie's 'Royal Scots' at Holbeck was not frequent, especially as late as June 1962. No 46105 *Cameron Highlander* was a long time resident of Polmadie, as far back as December 1933. It probably acted as a substitute for a failure during the previous night of one of the up sleepers, and was diagrammed to return on the 10.35am to Glasgow St Enoch, which was worked by Corkerhill men. It is shown just about to leave the depot for the station on 5 June 1962.

Above:
During the 1960s until the closure of the depot to steam, 'Britannias' were frequent visitors. Holbeck had had an allocation of three which were exchanged for 'Royal Scots' in 1959, whilst in the early 1950s No 70016 *Ariel* spent a short spell at the depot. Nearly all the 'Britannias' were allocated to Carlisle Kingmoor as they were displaced by diesels around the country. Shown in unlined green livery, although there is little sign of green paint on the boiler, No 70003 formerly named *John Bunyan* is outside No 1 shed before backing off the depot to work the 12.55pm Stourton-Carlisle freight on 15 October 1965. The emblem on the tender is much smaller than normal.

40181
40181

42394

40148

42616

Top Left:
In the days when the local passenger services in the Holbeck area were steam worked, the Stanier 2-6-2Ts were a common sight. By the early 1960s there were only a few left in the area, one of which was No 40181 allocated to Normanton and which could usually be seen working Normanton-Sowerby Bridge local trains, and occasionally trains to Leeds. The locomotive is shown on the ash pits on 16 June 1961.

Top Right:
Many of the Fowler 2-6-4Ts were a familiar sight around the West Riding of Yorkshire for at least 20 years and Holbeck had a small allocation for working expresses between Leeds and Bradford Forster Square and local services to Ilkley. A surprise transfer to Holbeck around 1963, from as far away as Swansea was No 42394 in recently ex-works condition. It is shown outside No 2 shed on 12 July 1964 and was withdrawn in June 1966, a real loss to preservation.

Bottom Leftt:
Five members of the class of 139 Stanier '3P' tanks were fitted with larger boilers during the early years of World War 2, in an attempt to improve their indifferent performance. It had, however, little effect on the locomotives and one of those modified, No 40148, was a Normanton locomotive by the early 1960s and is shown on the Holbeck ash pit.

Bottom Right:
The Stanier 2-6-4Ts were not seen at Holbeck very frequently in the 1960s, whilst the Fairburn versions were common. No 42616 allocated to Low Moor was on the depot on 6 June 1967, having been recently transferred from the Birkenhead area after the end of steam passenger workings in that district earlier in the year.

Above:
As mentioned previously, three 'Britannias' were exchanged for two 'Royal Scots' Nos 46103 and 46133 in October 1959. The three locomotives were Nos 70044 *Earl Haig*, No 70053 *Moray Firth*, and No 70054 *Dornoch Firth*. No 70044 arrived from Longsight depot at Manchester and was one of the two delivered new in 1953 fitted with Westinghouse air brake compressors, which prevented the fitting of smoke deflectors; this equipment was later removed.

As can be seen, the locomotive was fitted with one of the smaller tenders with a seven-ton coal capacity, as compared with Nos 70053 and 70054 which had the larger version with nine tons, and I am told that if the driver was over enthusiastic in the earlier stages of the journey from Leeds to Glasgow, the fireman faced a long walk to the back of the tender to find the coal by the time the train was leaving Kilmarnock. I often wondered why I bothered taking colour slides of locomotives in such a terrible external condition, but at least the headboard shows a little colour. *Earl Haig* is ready to leave the depot on 13 September 1960 to work the down 'Thames Clyde Express'.

44767
44916

Left:
Class 5 No 44767 was unique among the 842 members of the class as it was the only one to be fitted with Stephenson link motion. Other, though not unique, features were Timken roller bearings and double blastpipe and chimney, which was later removed. Happily the locomotive is preserved and has been a regular main line performer over the last 15 years. It was allocated to Bank Hall Liverpool for many years and worked the trans-Pennine services to Leeds and Bradford via the Calder Valley route, where I believe it had the reputation of being a strong locomotive. After these services were dieselised in 1961, the locomotive eventually became allocated to Carlisle Kingmoor, which meant it was a regular visitor to the Leeds area especially on freight workings over the Settle and Carlisle line.

During June 1967 an unofficial transfer was arranged by the respective district motive power superintendents whereby No 44767 was exchanged for a short period with one of the Holbeck Class 5s as the local superintendent, by the name of Tom Greaves, who was very much a steam enthusiast was curious to find out how No 44767 compared with the other locomotives. I never found out what conclusions if any were reached, but at least this little exercise allowed me to obtain several pictures of No 44767 working in the Leeds area.

It is shown inside No 2 shed, alongside No 44916 of Stockport on 15 June 1967 in rather dirty external condition. This was quickly rectified a few days later either by the efforts of the shed staff or local enthusiasts.

Below:
One of the workings on which No 44767 was regularly employed during its exchange period was the 12.50pm freight from Stourton to Carlisle. On 14 June 1967 it was photographed on this working as it entered Newlay cutting, five miles north of Leeds.

Above:
This was the last occasion that I saw a Midland 4-4-0 piloting one of the Scottish expresses. The locomotive is No 40685 which was allocated for these duties for many years, but judging by its external and probably mechanical condition as well, it was an incentive to drivers to try and go it alone rather than seeking its assistance. I well remember talking to a Holbeck driver at Carlisle, after I had travelled north on one of the sleepers, who had taken assistance from Hellifield as he had 'Jubilee' No 45569 *Tasmania* with a heavy train in winter. The driver complained that he had had to push it all the way to Blea Moor and then had a very uncomfortable high speed run to Carlisle to keep time.

The 'Royal Scot' being assisted and looking externally no better than the '2P' is No 46109 *Royal Engineer* and the date 28 May 1960. The '2Ps' seemed to last longer than the 'Compounds' on these duties, No 40491 being one of the last at Holbeck, and No 40613 at Carlisle Kingmoor.

Right:
Rebuilt 'Scot' No 46113 *Cameronian*, spent 10 of its last 11 years of service allocated to Holbeck depot; it is listed as having arrived in May 1951. It would be interesting to see a record of its visits to Crewe Works, and especially those of its tender, as the latter never received the final emblem. It was one of the few rebuilt 'Scots' to do any revenue earning work after it left Holbeck for Low Moor in 1961. In fact in May 1962 it was borrowed by Holbeck and used on the evening Morecambe residential service, before being withdrawn in December that year.

On 27 June 1961, it is shown on the depot ready to work the down 'Waverley', demonstrating another example of the only indication of colour on the transparency being the headboard.

THE
WAVERLEY

Above:
It was probably at the introduction of the summer timetable in 1961 that the 'Peaks' were first diagrammed for the down 'Thames-Clyde Express'. On 27 June 1961 No D31, later to become No 45030 and allocated to Holbeck for many years, is shown at Leeds City waiting to take over the down train.

Fairburn 2-6-4T No 42141 of Manningham is ready to depart with the morning Bristol Temple Meads-Bradford Forster Square train on the last leg of its journey.

Right:
Although 'Jubilee' No 45593 *Kolhapur* had still another year to work before withdrawal, it was on 19 September 1966 that the late Pat Whitehouse travelled on the locomotive from Leeds City — a trip which resulted in it being bought for preservation. The train was the afternoon van train to Wavertree at Liverpool, and it travelled via Standedge collecting vans *en route*.

I never regard *Kolhapur* as one of the proper Holbeck 'Jubilees', as it only arrived from the Western division in early 1966 and spent around 18 months at the depot. For no more than sentimental reasons I would have much preferred to have seen No 45562 *Alberta* selected for preservation, but apparently its tyres were well worn, or even No 45565 *Victoria* which had been withdrawn from Low Moor because it needed a new ash pan! — both locomotives had spent at least 25 years at Holbeck. Anyway, as is now well known, sentiment rather than mechanical condition can prove very expensive in the world of preservation and one should be thankful that there are still three operational 'Jubilees' in preservation.

45593

Above:
Unrebuilt 'Patriots' were rare visitors to Holbeck in the 1950s and 1960s until Lancaster received the last members of the class to work out their days on the Morecambe trains. An allocation list for 1945 shows Nos 5534, 5535 and 5538 still at the depot, even after the arrival of four rebuilt 'Scots', as well as 22 'Jubilees'. They must have been transferred away soon after this date.

This unusual picture shows No 45507 *Royal Tank Corps* together with an unlikely visitor in the shape of 'A3' Pacific No 60096 *Papyrus* of Haymarket which had arrived with an up Scottish express, no doubt covering for a 'Peak' failure on 9 April 1962. It was an interesting week at the depot as it was also visited by 'A3' 60052 *Prince Palatine* from Gateshead, and Peppercorn 'A2' No 60534 *Irish Elegance.*

Below:
Holbeck depot was allocated Class 5s Nos 44755-57 from new in April 1948 and they remained at the depot until withdrawal between November 1963 and November 1965, except for No 44757 which was actually withdrawn from Southport. They were fitted with Caprotti Valve gear, timken roller bearings throughout, and double chimney and were initially used on the Scottish expresses to the north. This did not appear to last very long as the Caprotti locomotives didn't seem to perform well on the hills, so from my observation they normally seemed to be employed south of Leeds. They were very unattractive machines, and I don't think the double chimney really gave any advantages over the single. No 44755 is shown on the depot on 21 September 1960.

Above:
It is hard to believe that the standard blue livery was being applied to diesels more than two years before steam finished on British Rail in August 1968.

On the 16 March 1967 'Peak' No D30 (later No 45029) still in green can be compared with No D55 (later No 45144) *Royal Signals* on the ash pits at the depot. In the background is the preserved Johnson Midland '1F' 0-6-0T No 41708, the only one of the 280 in the class to survive. It was bought for preservation after its working days at Stanton and Staveley finished in around 1965. It was in the yard on blocks while its tyres and axleboxes received attention before eventually going to the Keighley & Worth Valley Railway.

Above:
There were only 25 of the 2-10-0 Austerities, and with the exception of No 90763, which was based at Carlisle Kingmoor, the rest of the class worked north of the border, shared between Carstairs, Motherwell, Polmadie and Grangemouth depots. No 90763 occasionally ventured as far south as Hellifield, but 19 July 1962 was only the second occasion I ever saw it as far south as Holbeck. Three members of the class were withdrawn in 1961, and the rest in 1962. No 90763 succumbed, along with many others, in December. I later photographed it in October 1963 at Darlington Shed awaiting scrap.

1N20
D9005

Left:
Completely dwarfed by the massive 300-ton capacity coaler, Gateshead-allocated 'Deltic' No D9005 *The Prince of Wales' Own Regiment of Yorkshire*, looking nearly as dirty as some of the steam locomotives, reverses towards the fuelling point having worked one of the evening expresses from King's Cross. In the background is a Class 03 shunter.

Above:
A general view taken on 1 June 1966 shows the terrible state into which the shed yard had got by the mid-1960s, whilst the external state of 2-8-0 '8F' No 48283 and Fairburn 2-6-4T No 42052, both Holbeck locomotives, does little to alleviate the air of decline. The Type 4 diesel No D1611 (later Nos 47032, 47662 and 47817) looks very out of place surrounded by all the coal and dirt. In the background can be seen the signalbox on the main line which controlled the entrance to the depot.

GRADE
1
GRADE
2
45660
55
A

Left:
'Jubilee' No 45660 *Rooke* under one of the 150-ton coal bunkers is receiving grade 1 coal if the notice is to be believed on 29 March 1965. This locomotive will always be remembered for the dynamometer car trials on the Settle-Carlisle line in October 1937, when some of the highest power outputs ever to be recorded with the class were achieved. It became allocated to Holbeck towards the end of 1964 to work up its mileage before being withdrawn in June 1966. No 45660 spent many postwar years allocated to Bristol Barrow Road Depot and was frequently in the Leeds area on workings such as the 'Devonian'.

Above:
Immingham-based 'B1' No 61406 was a regular visitor to the depot in the mid-1960s, working from Cleethorpes to Leeds. This locomotive was always well cleaned and is shown by the ashpit hoist on the road that led into Shed No 1. It will already have passed through the coal bunker and will call at the water column a few yards further on before returning to Leeds Central. After the closure of Copley Hill Depot (56C) in September 1964, locomotives that worked into Leeds Central came to Holbeck for servicing.
Also seen is another regular visitor to the depot — Class 5 No 44965 of Saltley recently ex-works from Crewe in its unlined black livery. No 61406 survived until April 1966 and No 44965 till March 1968. The date is 29 March 1965.

Above:
In the early 1960s British Rail ran special trains from Glasgow to London named 'Starlight Specials'. These trains left Glasgow on Friday night and offered very cheap fares and were very popular. This involved working empty stock north on Thursdays, and on 7 September 1961 two trains were run of 15 coaches each. Locomotives were changed at Whitehall Junction, Leeds.

The first train 3X46 headed north for Carlisle with Holbeck's '8F' No 48067, and if its external condition matched its mechanical, it would have been a lively journey for the crew. No doubt it would have been looped *en route* as it departed about half an hour before the down 'Waverley'. In the background is the 'Jubilee' which had brought in the morning train from Carnforth and is turning on the Whitehall triangle before returning on the 1.54pm. Also visible is Holbeck 'Britannia' No 70053 ready to take over the next empty stock train.

Right:
A comparison of the different fronts of two 2-10-0 '9Fs' side by side in the depot yard. On the left is ex-Crosti-boilered locomotive No 92024, whilst on the right is single chimney No 92101. The ex-Crosti-boilered locomotives rarely appeared at the depot until the last few years of steam operation when No 92024 and others were allocated to Carlisle Kingmoor and visited the area frequently. No 92101 based in Lancashire was probably waiting a return tank train working back to Stanlow. The date is 23 June 1967.

20424
N. E. LEEDS.HOLBECK

Above:
The arrival of Gresley 'A3s' at Holbeck was an unexpected and major event. They were only diagrammed for working north of Leeds, and were in the hands of drivers and firemen brought up on rebuilt 'Royal Scots' and 'Jubilees', but nevertheless the crews took to them very well indeed, liking the comfort of the cabs and their free steaming, although some of the locomotives had run up high mileages since last major overhauls. Nos 60077 *The White Knight* and 60038 *Firdausi* are recorded as being allocated on 27 February 1960 followed on 14 May by Nos 60080/82/88/92, all of which came from the Newcastle area. Later in the year on 26 November No 60069/70/72 arrived from Copley Hill. Never had Holbeck seen so much large motive power for working the Scottish expresses north, but in spite of having nine 'A3s' they still managed to 'borrow' the four 'A3s' allocated to Neville Hill. Although it must be said these locomotives had little to do and generally were in better condition than the new acquisitions.

Ready to leave the depot on 3 March 1961 is No 60082 *Neil Gow* to work the down 'Thames-Clyde Express'.

Right:
The Western Region and indeed the old Great Western Railway always had a tendency to do things differently from the other regions, and so in the latter years of steam they decided to paint all passenger locomotives in green, lined and unlined, from 0-4-2Ts upwards.

Standard 5MT No 73003 which was allocated to Barrow Road (82E) is on the ash pits after working an express from Bristol on 21 August 1961.

73003

Above:
From the illustrations on these two pages the reader could be forgiven for thinking the book was featuring an ex-LNER main line depot. Nevertheless the ex-Eastern and North Eastern Region Pacifics, not to mention those from the Scottish Region, were frequent visitors to the depot in the mid-1960s, especially after the closure of Copley Hill. Doncaster had a large allocation of 'A1s' with little to do on the main line, so they were used on the Leeds-Doncaster stopping trains. No 60157 *Great Eastern* visited the depot on 17 October 1964, only three months before its withdrawal. It was one of the last batch built at Doncaster in November 1949, and was one of five in the class to be fitted with Timken roller bearings.

Above:
12 April 1962 saw a rare visitor when Peppercorn 'A2' No 60534 *Irish Elegance* arrived on a working from the north during the previous night. This was the only occasion I saw one of these locomotives on the depot. Built in May 1948 it was allocated to York, but departed for Haymarket in November 1949 where it remained until November 1961, spending its last year at St Margarets. Its external condition is in sharp contrast to the way it was kept in the 1950s. Also visible is Gateshead 'A3' No 60052 *Prince Palatine*, which had been borrowed by Holbeck during the week to work the 'Waverley' to Carlisle. This was the last 'A3' to be withdrawn from St Margarets Depot in January 1966.

Above:
The Gresley 'V2s' were not seen at the depot as frequently as the Pacifics, but on 2 February 1964 No 60887 is in the yard. Based at York it was withdrawn five months after the photograph was taken. I do remember seeing on the shed board one day, that a 'V2' had been diagrammed to haul a freight over the Settle and Carlisle line, but I have never seen any photographs of them on that line other than special workings.

Right:
This well-kept Immingham 'B1' No 61406 is also featured earlier. It is on the ash pits being serviced before making its return journey from Leeds Central to Cleethorpes on 11 June 1965.

61406
61406

Above:
'A3' Pacific No 60092 *Fairway* was one of the class to be transferred to Holbeck in May 1960 for working the Scottish expresses over the Settle and Carlisle line. The locomotives were transferred from Newcastle depots where they had been based for many years; in the case of No 60092, since January 1937. Most had run high mileages, and, with the exception of Nos 60038 and 60077, did not have visits to Doncaster for overhaul whilst allocated at Holbeck. No 60092 left in June 1961 for Ardsley. It must have been to the works before it became allocated to Gateshead again in June 1963, as it had by that date gained new deflectors. It would have done very little work before withdrawal in October 1964. It is on the depot on 15 May 1964 having worked a special to Leeds from the northeast.

Right:
Rebuilt 'Scot' No 46113 *Cameronian* spent 10 years at Holbeck from May 1951 to October 1961 when it was transferred to Low Moor. On 10 May 1962 it had obviously been borrowed by Holbeck to work the Leeds portion of the Morecambe evening residential, and is shown passing Crossflatts in fine style. This must have been one of its last main line passenger duties, as it was withdrawn in December. It is interesting to note it has a 56D shed plate, indicating it had been transferred from Low Moor to Mirfield. The tender retained the old style lion and wheel emblem to withdrawal.

46113

Left:
The most famous train worked by Holbeck Depot was the 'Thames-Clyde Express' for which it provided the motive power north of Leeds, and shared it with other main line Midland depots to and from St Pancras. These three pictures taken of the down train from the end of the platform at Leeds City, show the regular motive power which worked the train during steam operation since the end of World War 2. The Holbeck 'Britannias' were also regular performers, but unfortunately I did not obtain a photograph of one at this location. The up and down trains were booked to be in Leeds station together which caused confusion to many passengers who occasionally boarded the wrong train. On 28 February 1960, rebuilt 'Scot' No 46145 *The Duke of Wellington's Regt (West Riding)* was in charge.

Right:
On the previous Sunday to 28 February 1960 illustrated on the preceding page, the Holbeck crew were not so lucky, as they had been allocated 'Jubilee' No 45564 *New South Wales* for their journey to Glasgow St Enoch. I am sure they would have preferred a rebuilt 'Scot'. This locomotive is recorded as being allocated to Holbeck in 1945 and it remained at the depot until withdrawal in July 1964.

Far Right:
Neville Hill-allocated 'A3' No 60086 *Gainsborough* is ready to depart on 14 March 1961. It was allocated to Neville Hill from February 1949 to June 1961 and was employed working expresses such as the 'Queen of Scots' between Leeds and Newcastle. It did little work around this period as these workings had been dieselised, and was often 'borrowed' by Holbeck as it was in far better condition than the latter's own locomotives. It was finally withdrawn in November 1964 from Darlington.

THE
THAMES-CLYDE
EXPRESS
45564

60086
THE
THAMES-CLYDE
EXPRESS
A-3

Left:
Rebuilt 'Scot' No 46117 *Welsh Guardsman* rounds the sharp curve at Bingley Junction, Shipley, at the head of the up 'Waverley' express on 10 May 1961, a working which the locomotive must have done numerous times since it arrived at Holbeck after rebuilding in December 1943, and which it continued to do until just before its withdrawal in November 1962.

Right:
In 1960 and 1961 as the English Electric Type 4 diesels took over all the main line duties on the West Coast, many of the 'Scots', rebuilt 'Patriots' and 'Britannias' which had been allocated to depots such as Camden, Longsight, Crewe North and others, for many years had no work, and so were transferred to the the Midland main line. As a result depots which had relied on 'Jubilees' for their main line duties received Class 7 power. In this picture rebuilt 'Patriot' No 45522 *Prestatyn* hauls the 12.35pm express to St Pancras out of Leeds City. This locomotive was the last of the 'Patriots' to be rebuilt (in 1949). It was finally withdrawn in 1964. The date is 28 August 1961.

45522

Above:
Holbeck-based Fowler 2-6-4T No 42409 is caught looking immaculate in No 2 shed. The locomotive had been specially prepared to work a Railway Correspondence & Travel Society special the next day. Called 'The Nidd Valley' the train was the last train to travel the Pateley Bridge branch. The locomotive along with 20 other members of the class was withdrawn the following year. The date is 18 October 1963.

Right:
Holbeck depot was to close to steam around six weeks after this fine night picture was taken in No 1 shed, showing the immaculate condition the last 'Jubilees' were kept by the shed staff with help from the local enthusiasts. No 45593 *Kolhapur* and 45562 *Alberta* await their next duties on 12 August 1967. These would most likely be a rail tour, or a trip to Carlisle on a Saturday. *D. C. Rogers*

45593
45562

42689

Left:
An unlikely trio lined up inside No 2 roundhouse in 1967. On the left is local Fairburn tank No 42689, but in the centre is the preserved 2-4-0 Midland Kirtley Class 156 No 158A, which became No 20002 in the LMS numbering. Built in 1866, rebuilt in 1881 and 1897, it lasted until July 1947, when it was restored at Derby Works, and is now part of the National Collection. The looks of the Class 08 shunter are in stark contrast to the elegant lines of the Midland machine. The Kirtley was probably *en route* to or from Hellifield. The date is 20 August 1967.

Right:
Holbeck depot was one of the sheds which over the latter years of steam received much attention from photographers who wanted to capture the magic of the light and shade which it offered. Whilst this was relatively easy to do with black and white film, it was much more difficult with the slide films available at the time. The lighting and atmosphere are well captured in this picture of a Standard '9F' Class 5 inside No 1 shed on 18 February 1967. *D. C. Rogers*

Above:
Class 5 No 44726 of Kingmoor depot, inside No 2 shed on 29 August 1963 alongside 'Jubilee' No 45631 *Tanganyika* which was allocated to Burton-on-Trent, mainly for working freight traffic. Several of the class finished their days at Burton Depot on mundane duties. It was withdrawn a year after this picture was taken. The Class 5 was one of the locomotives built with steel fireboxes during 1949 at Crewe. The locomotive spent most of, if not all, of its time allocated to Kingmoor and was withdrawn in 1966.

Right:
A glimpse from inside No 1 roundhouse through the entrance showing 'Britannia' No 70021 *Morning Star* parked in the yard. Built in August 1951 the locomotive spent many years on the Western Region and, as can be seen, did not have the hand-rails removed from the smoke deflectors. Like most members of the class it finished its working days on the LM Region, being withdrawn in December 1967. The photograph was taken on 6 September 1967.

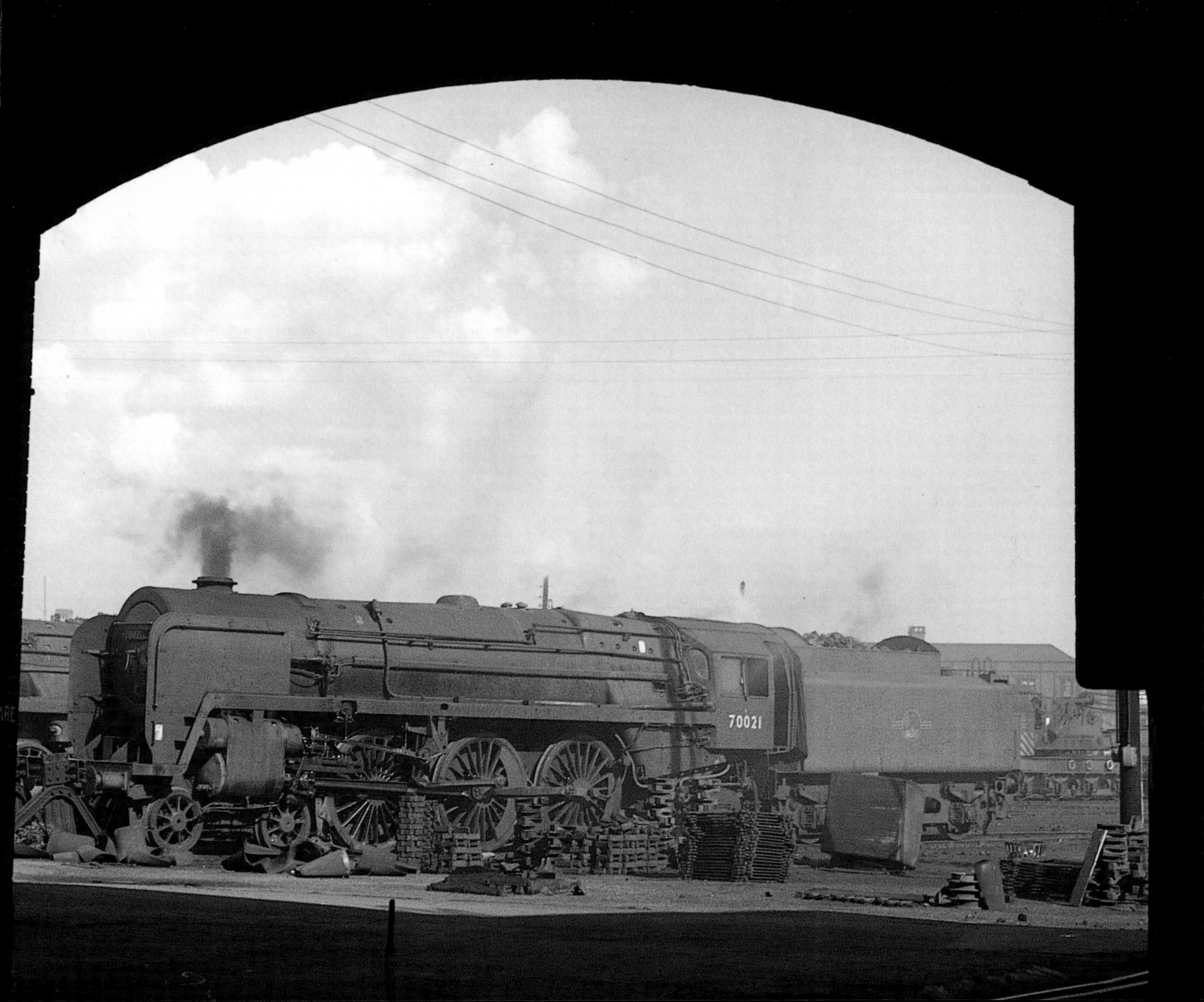
70021

Above:
The date of this photograph is 30 September 1967 — the day that Holbeck closed to steam operation. To mark the occasion the West Riding branch of the RCTS organised a brake-van trip from Stourton to Carlisle on the 1.30pm working, with Holbeck's long-time resident 'Jubilee' No 45562 *Alberta* in immaculate condition. About an hour earlier ex-GWR 'Castle' class No 7029 *Clun Castle* had passed on its famous special from Peterborough to Carlisle. I decided that I would follow *Alberta* rather than the 'Castle' which proved a good move as I managed to get 16 different action shots as far as Ribblehead viaduct, not bad value by today's standards.

Right:
Although this picture suggests otherwise, it was in fact the last day of steam operation at Holbeck, and was taken from up the coaling tower. I cannot understand why, but this was the only occasion I photographed from this excellent position. There is a selection of diesels on view — Classes 24, 25, 40, 46 and 47 all surprisingly clean — with immaculate local Class 5 No 45428 now preserved on the North Yorkshire Moors Railway.

A63
3E 05
45428

Left:
Prior to its famous rail tour duties on the East Coast main line, and over the Settle-Carlisle and Shap routes, *Clun Castle* carried out clearance trials. On 21 August 1967 it travelled from Doncaster to Leeds, and then northwards to the Skipton area, after which it arrived back at Holbeck in the evening for servicing. It is shown on the ashpits after being coaled; notice it is without its nameplates or numberplates.

Right:
Probably the most unusual visitor I ever saw on Holbeck was the veteran Highland 'Jones Goods' No 103 on 25 May 1964. It was returning north from Bedford, where it had been employed on the line to Hitchin during the making of the film *Those Magnificent Men in their Flying Machines*, when it was disguised as a French engine, carrying number 23 and 'Nord' on the tender. Built in June 1894 by Sharp Stewart it worked the Highland line for most of its days until withdrawn in October 1934. It was repainted in Highland livery and then disappeared from public view into St Rollox Works paint shop, until it was dumped outside during the war, causing deterioration. It re-entered the paint shop in 1946 and was again repainted and there it remained until the Scottish General Manager, Mr James Ness, decided in 1958 to return the locomotive to working order for special tours. It operated extensively until being placed in the Glasgow Museum of Transport on 6 July 1966. It was only due to the shed staff moving the locomotive for me, that I was able to obtain this picture, and I was the only photographer around. Presumably the locomotive headed north over the Settle-Carlisle line the following day.

OMOO

Left:
A study of ancient and modern on 16 March 1967 — 82 years separate the building dates of Midland '1F' 0-6-0T No 41708, with that of English Electric Type 3 (later Class 37) No D6786 in December 1962. The Midland tank had been placed on blocks whilst it had attention to its wheels prior to going to the Worth Valley Railway. It was in fact the last of the class of 240 to be withdrawn, although it survived along with four others much longer than the rest of the class, due to a 100-year agreement between the Iron Works at Staveley and the Midland Railway made in 1866. The other four locomotives were scrapped. It is now working on the Swanage Railway. No D6786, which became No 37086 and later No 37516 is still hard at work from Immingham depot.

Left:
Bulleid Light Pacific No 34051 (ex No 21C151) *Winston Churchill* had been chosen by the National Railway Museum for preservation. Built in December 1946 it covered 807,496 miles before withdrawal in September 1965. Two months later it was dragged north to be stored in Hellifield Shed, and on 10 December 1965 it paused on Holbeck Depot. It was accompanied by Standard 5MT No 73112 *Morgan le Fay* which was *en route* to Rotherham for scrap, but somehow didn't get detached during the journey and arrived at Holbeck. *Winston Churchill* is currently at the NRM at York, but is unlikely to be put into working order as there are many others of the class which are preserved and currently in working order. *Morgan le Fey* was, however, not to escape the scrapman for long.

Above:
It has not been my intention to include many pictures of the current preserved locomotives which have frequently visited Holbeck in recent years, as these are well documented in other publications. I felt I couldn't exclude this historic picture of the day when the original Johnson 'Compound' No 1000, although in its modified Deeley form, visited its old depot for the first time in many years to be prepared for the Cumbrian Rail Tour on 4 September 1960. Those who were lucky enough to be on this memorable day out, are not likely to forget the sound from the locomotive as it breasted Ais Gill summit at 30 mph with its nine coach train, not to mention the 88mph maximum on the descent through Settle station. Currently at the NRM at York, although not operational, it is hoped we may see it out on the main lines again in the future.

62005
52
H

Left:
During its working life with British Rail 'K1' No 62005 carried out royal train duties on two occasions. The last was in 1967 when it hauled the royal train from Newcastle Central to its stabling point to provide steam heat. Later it carried out a 195-mile Stephenson Locomotive Society tour on 20 May, and after further duties at Newcastle it was retired to Holbeck depot while its future was considered. It is shown in No 2 roundhouse on 29 September 1967 complete with copper capped chimney! By the year end it was back at Thornaby, and then carried out stationary boiler duties at Phillips Oil Refinery from which it eventually returned much the worse for wear. It then went to Neville Hill Depot at Leeds for several years, until it was bought by the North Eastern Locomotive Preservation Group in May 1972. Since then it has travelled extensively on British Rail, and become a firm favourite on the West Highland line.

Above:
No doubt many of the Clayton Type 1 (Class 17) diesels passed Holbeck, or visited the depot when on delivery to Scotland, but 5 October 1962 was the only occasion that I observed one.

Looking immaculate *en route* to Polmadie Depot at Glasgow to start its six years of use, it was withdrawn by October 1968, and finally cut up at BREL Glasgow in January 1973. These locomotives, all 117 of them, must have been among the most expensive disasters of the modernisation scheme, all having been withdrawn by the end of 1971.

Left:
The Metropolitan Vickers Type 2 Co-Bo Class 28s passed Holbeck daily in their early years when working the famous 'Condor' night express freight from London to Scotland, but were seldom seen on the depot. On 9 September 1965, No D5705 had arrived hauling 'Jubilee' No 45726 *Vindictive en route* for scrapping. The 'Jubilee' had been withdrawn the previous March. No D5705, built in December 1958, lasted until September 1968 when it was transferred to Departmental Stock, and then fortunately it passed into preservation. It is currently under lengthy restoration at Matlock in Derbyshire.

Right:
Just in case readers of this book were under the impression that express steam locomotives were always kept in the immaculate condition we have become used to with preservation, I thought I would include this picture of 'Britannia' No 70028 *Royal Star* of Crewe North taken on 25 March 1965.

Sights such as these, which were very common, did very little to encourage colour photography, hence I concentrated on black and white. The locomotive lasted until September 1967, so it must have been in better condition than it appeared. It was of course, originally one of the batch allocated to Cardiff Canton for working the Paddington express in the early 1950s and at that time would have been kept in immaculate condition.

Above:
The Stanier Moguls ('5P4F') were seen much more frequently at Farnley Junction Depot in Leeds rather than Holbeck where they were not common, but on 21 April 1961 No 42969 was in the yard. The class was normally to be found in the 1950s and 1960s working around Crewe, Birkenhead, Birmingham and over Shap. No 42969 was one of the earlier withdrawals of the class in 1964, the last going in 1967.

Right:
'Q6' 0-8-0s were allocated to Neville Hill Depot at Leeds for some time and worked to Kippax and Stourton, and were frequently seen passing the depot. In June 1966 they were transferred to Normanton before being moved back to the northeast in October 1966. They occasionally visited Holbeck after Neville Hill became part of the '55' area for repairs and No 63420 was photographed in the yard on 25 March 1965. Several of these excellent locomotives, built between 1913 and 1921, survived until September 1967, and one is now preserved on the North Yorkshire Moors Railway.

63420
63420

Above:
Passing Bingley Junction, Shipley, on 10 May 1961 the down 'Thames-Clyde Express' was worked by 'A3' No 60082 *Neil Gow* which spent 14 months allocated to Holbeck from May 1960 to July 1961, when it returned to the northeast, where it was usually allocated during its 39-year working career.

Top Right:
The up 'Waverley' approaches Apperley Bridge on a hot day in June 1962, headed up 'Jubilee' No 45565 *Victoria* looking very smart in its lined green livery after its recent, and last, visit to Crewe for a major overhaul. A long-time resident of Holbeck, it was in fact transferred to Low Moor for its last couple of years, and became a favourite with the local enthusiasts, working from Bradford to Blackpool via Copy Pit on summer Saturdays. Its eventual reason for withdrawal in January 1967 was because it needed a new ash pan! The fourth vehicle in the train was a 12-wheel dining car.

Bottom Right:
The last occasion that I saw a Holbeck rebuilt 'Scot' working the 'Thames-Clyde Express' was on 6 June 1961, when No 46145 *The Duke of Wellington's Regiment (West Riding)* was photographed passing Apperley Bridge with the down train. The locomotive was rebuilt in January 1944 and arrived at Holbeck in January 1953. It was transferred away soon after this date on paper to Low Moor but was stored at Farnley Junction.

Left:
Having just arrived at Carlisle after my first footplate trip on the 'Thames-Clyde Express'. On 20 August 1960, I just had time to capture this picture of 'A3' No 60082 *Neil Gow* as it took water before setting off north, for the first stop at Dumfries. It was a never to be forgotten experience, a superb piece of driving by Tommy Warren ably assisted by fireman Les Simpson. Thirteen minutes were gained on schedule without excessively high speed, as Inspector Albert Pullan was also on board. The locomotive steamed and rode superbly which was in sharp contrast to the rather rough 'Royal Scot' we had on the return trip.

Right:
Rebuilt 'Scot' No 46162 *Queens Westminster Rifleman* is ready to leave the depot on 23 September 1960 to take over the up 'Thames-Clyde Express', being allocated to Kentish Town Depot (14B). Rebuilt in April 1948, it was finally withdrawn in June 1964. Undoubtedly the most important event during its career was when it was chosen as one of the locomotives to take part in the 1948 Locomotive Exchanges, where together with No 46154 *The Hussar* it put up some of the finest performances of the Exchanges.

THE THAMES-CLYDE EXPRESS
46162
46162

Above:
Carlisle United Football Club nearly always did well in the FA Cup in the early 1960s, and the Carlisle depots always responded by cleaning the locomotives rostered to the specials for away matches. On 25 January 1964, two trains were run from Carlisle to, I believe, Luton. Rebuilt 'Jubilee' No 45736 *Phoenix* and rebuilt 'Patriot' No 45527 *Southport* were selected for the specials and were cleaned, even though there was little green paint left on the locomotives. The 'Jubilee' was withdrawn in September and the 'Patriot' during 1964. After rebuilding in 1942 the two rebuilt 'Jubilees' were used with great success on the Leeds-Glasgow trains, being allocated to Holbeck.

Below:
Undoubtedly the most remarkable steam working in 1967 was as a result of the decision by the District Motive Power Superintendent to use steam on a Royal Train.

The Duke of Edinburgh was being taken to Nidd Bridge north of Harrogate, and Holbeck's 'Jubilee' No 45562 *Alberta* was selected as the train engine, with Class 5 No 45428 as the stand-by. The engine was really cleaned up as can be seen in this picture of the train passing Wormald Green on 30 May 1967 *en route* to turn at Ripon, which was by then the end of the line. Superb as *Alberta* appeared, it must be said that the Class 5 was even smarter.

45428

Left:
The day after the royal train working, stand-by loco Class 5 No 45428 simmers gently on the shed, not having been called to the royal train. The locomotive continued active until steam ended in the West Riding four months after this event. It passed into preservation, and is now at the North Yorkshire Moors Railway and named *Eric Treacy.* It has never carried out main line duties in preservation.

Above:
The last of the unrebuilt 'Patriots' were withdrawn in 1962. In the late 1950s and very early 1960s, Bristol Barrow Road Depot had three of the class allocated, Nos 45504, 45506 and 45519, which were frequently seen at York and Leeds, usually working the 'Devonian' express. Waiting for its next duty back to Bristol on 29 June 1960 was *Royal Signals* in the sidings on the depot. In 1945 Holbeck had three numbers of the class allocated: Nos 5534, 5535, 5538.

Above:
Another view in the yard around the ash pits. 'Jubilee' No 45562 *Alberta* in its usual immaculate condition during the last year of Holbeck steam, contrasts sharply with King moor 'Britannia' No 70005, originally named *John Milton*. The picture was taken on 6 June 1967 when there was only three months to go before closure to steam. The 'Britannia' was withdrawn the following month after 16 years' service, compared to the 33 years of *Alberta.*

Right:
The Carlisle Kingmoor-based 'Clans' Nos 72005-72009 were frequent visitors to Leeds on passenger and freight workings over the Settle-Carlisle line, whereas the Polmadie locos were seldom seen.

Although the 'Clans' have gone down in history as not really matching up to what was expected of them, I personally regarded them as the best looking of the Standard designs. No 72006 *Clan Mackintosh* is on the ash pit waiting to be serviced on 21 August 1960. This was the last member of the class to survive, and was withdrawn in May 1966 after just over 14 years of service.

72006
CLAN MACKENZIE
72006

Above:
Seen from the side of the coaler on 13 April 1969 is local 'Jubilee' No 45568 *Western Australia*, another locomotive that spent over 20 years at the depot, being withdrawn in April 1964. Alongside is Saltley-based Class 5 No 44814 a frequent visitor at the time; behind is a Standard Class 9F 2-10-0.

Right:
'Jubilee' No 45647 *Sturdee* looking well-cleaned in spite of the fact it was withdrawn within the month. It is heading the Bradford Forster Square-Heysham vans past Coniston Cold between Gargrave and Belle Busk on 18 March 1967.

45647

Above:
A line-up of sharp contrast: shown in the yard on 19 June 1967 are Fairburn 2-6-4T No 42689, 'Jubilee' No 45562 *Alberta* and ex-Crosti-boilered 2-10-0 No 92021 of Carlisle Kingmoor, and Class 5 No 45072 in the background. The '9F' was withdrawn in December 1967 from Birkenhead.

Right:
'Jubilee' No 45636 *Uganda*, of Leicester Depot (15C), pulls out of Leeds City on 20 August 1960 at the head of the up 'Thames-Clyde Express'. The locomotive has a red background to the nameplate. It was withdrawn in December 1962 along with 41 other members of the class during the year. This working was normally undertaken by a Kentish Town or Holbeck locomotive at this time.

THE THAMES-CLYDE EXPRESS
45636
42093
45636

70024

Left:
A busy scene viewed just to the south of the depot on 1 May 1967, with the top of the coaler visible above the bridge. Two dirty Class 25s prepare to go north, whilst 'Britannia' No 70024 formerly named *Vulcan* is ready to haul the 12.55pm ex-Stourton Yard to Carlisle, a common working for a 'Britannia' at this time. No 70024 lasted until the end of steam at Kingmoor in December 1967.

Right:
The day before the depot was closed to steam operation, 29 September 1967, 'Jubilee' No 45593 *Kolhapur* was positioned at the entrance to No 1 shed, still in very clean condition. As history will record, Holbeck continued as a diesel centre for a further 26 years, until the final locomotives departed on Saturday 2 October 1993, except for some derelict Class 47s.

Above:
Holbeck carried on as a main diesel depot after the steam finished on 30 September 1967, with an allocation of 'Peaks', Class 47s, Class 25s and 08s. The steam buildings were demolished in 1970 and diesel servicing facilities erected. A general view across the yard on 8 October 1990 shows Class 37 No 37421, recently transferred to Immingham after several years' service at Inverness. In the background is Class 47 No 47564 *Colossus*, which has recently lost its name and been repainted in the current Rail Express Systems (Res) red livery.

The viaduct in the background used to carry the line to Dewsbury and Huddersfield, before it was changed to form part of the route to Wakefield Westgate and Doncaster, before eventual closure. The washing plants are seen at either side of No 47564, and the fuelling point is out of the picture on the right.

Below:
When Class 25 No 25322 was withdrawn from Crewe Depot, it was stored in Basford Hall yard, as apparently it had no defects. It was eventually moved to Tinsley Yard, where it stayed for three days before being taken in a train to Holbeck, and placed inside the repair shop. It was now owned by the training department at York. There it remained for a considerable time, before it was unofficially adopted by four BR employees who over a six to seven month period gave the locomotive a 'D' exam. The work was carried out in their spare time. Minor items had been removed from the locomotive after withdrawal, but the major work carried out was to the injectors. Three piston liners had new heads, electrical equipment was overhauled and the bogie equipment was repaired. This put the locomotive into a condition fit for main line running. After a test trip to Skipton with ecs, it was allowed to work rail tours, until 30 March 1991 when it ran a special to Holyhead for the last time.

When this picture was taken on 28 April 1991, the locomotive (as No 7672) was ready to leave the depot for the last time under its own power to go to Glasgow for the removal of asbestos, before passing into preservation.

It was because no sector of BR was prepared to sponsor the locomotive that it was sold, and it passed to preservation in first class working order. Other classes visible in the picture are 37, 31, 47, and 08.

Left:
A line up of locomotives in the sidings next to the main line awaiting their next duties on 6 July 1990.

On the left is Class 31 No 31400 (originally No 31161 and No D5579) and now withdrawn, with Class 47 No 47533 behind, which was one of the early members of the class to be painted red. It had a premature end due to a head-on collision with No 47472 at Reading on 12 February 1991, both locomotives being withdrawn. In the next line is the unique Class 140 unit, built in 1981 and numbered 55500 based on a Leyland National bus body. This unit lay out of use for many years on the depot. In front is ex-Scottish Class 47 No 47597 with large Scottie-dog logo, a feature of Eastfield depot in Glasgow. On the right is Class 47 No 47234 in grey freight livery, but without symbols, and in the far right a couple of 08s.

Leeds Holbeck Locomotive Allocations

Allocation at 1945

MR '2P' 4-4-0	432, 455, 489, 519, 562
LMS '2P' 4-4-0	567, 633
MR '3P' 4-4-0	720, 725, 736, 748, 758, 759
MR '4P' 4-4-0	1018, 1040
LMS '4P' 4-4-0	910, 927, 928, 1069, 1087, 1117, 1137, 1144
MR '1P' 0-4-4T	1247, 1315, 1422
MR '1P' 0-6-0T	1745

Allocation at 1945

'Crab' 2-6-0	2850
MR '3F' 0-6-0	3401, 3665
MR '4F' 0-6-0	3878, 4020
LMS '4F' 0-6-0	4044, 4151, 4431, 4501
Stanier '5MT' 4-6-0	4820, 4821, 4823, 4824, 4828, 4847, 4848, 4849, 4850, 4853, 4854, 4856, 4857, 5040, 5043, 5092, 5093, 5187, 5260, 5276, 5280, 5289
'Patriot' 4-6-0	5534, 5535, 5538
'Jubilee' 4-6-0	5558, 5562, 5565, 5568, 5569, 5587, 5589, 5594, 5597, 5598, 5604, 5605, 5608, 5611, 5619, 5620, 5648, 5651, 5658, 5659, 5660, 5694
'Royal Scot' 4-6-0	6103, 6108, 6109, 6117
MR '3F' 0-6-0T	7254
LMS '3F' 0-6-0T	7418
Stanier '8F' 2-8-0	8001, 8073, 8090, 8110, 8121, 8124, 8126, 8127, 8128, 8129, 8137, 8138, 8143, 8176, 8177, 8306
L & YR '2P' 2-4-2T	10622, 10630, 10634, 10689, 10880

Locomotives on the depot on 8 Sept 1954

LMS '3P' 2-6-2T	40169, 40163
Mid '3P' 4-4-0	40323, 40521
Mid '4P' 4-4-0	41065, 41068, 41100, 41104, 41196, 41197
LMS '2P' 2-6-2T	41267
LMS '4P' 2-6-4T	42685
LMS '5P/4F' 2-6-0	42774, 42855
LMS '4MT' 2-6-0	43113, 43117
LMS '3F' 0-6-0	43225, 43770
LMS '4F' 0-6-0	43953, 44171, 44404, 44501, 44550
LMS '5MT' 4-6-0	44662, 44672, 44826, 44828, 44842, 44843, 44849, 44898, 44916, 45081, 45264, 45375
'Jubilee' 4-6-0	45562, 45605, 45694, 45739
'Royal Scot' 4-6-0	46113, 46117, 46133
LMS '2MT' 2-6-0	46493, 46498
LMS '3F' 0-6-0T	47254, 47418, 47470
LMS '8F' 2-8-0	48154, 48157, 48283, 48399, 48448
BR '5MT' 4-6-0	73015

Locomotives on the depot on 21 Oct 1956

LMS '3P' 2-6-2T	40169, 40193
Mid '3P' 4-4-0	40491
Mid '4P' 4-4-0	41071, 41108, 41100
LMS '2P' 2-6-2T	41267
LMS '4P' 2-6-4T	42377
LMS '5MT' 2-6-0	42771, 42795, 42884
LMS '4MT' 2-6-0	43039, 43117
LMS '4F' 0-6-0	43843, 43968, 44039, 44501
LMS '5MT' 4-6-0	44662, 44756, 44757, 44826, 45056, 45059, 45273, 45285

LMS '5XP' 4-6-0	45554, 45562, 45565, 45573, 45576, 45608, 45658, 45663
'Royal Scot' 4-6-0	46113, 46117
LMS '2MT; 2-6-0	46993
LMS '3F' 0-6-0T	47254, 47418
LMS '8F' 2-8-0	48158, 48159, 48283, 48472, 48542
BR '5MT' 4-6-0	73073, 73069

Locomotives m the depot on Wednesday 1 September 1959

LMS '3P' 2-6-2T	40148 *stored*
LMS '3P' 4-4-0	40491, 40552 *stored*
LMS '5MT' 2-6-0	42835
LMS '4F' 0-6-0	44576
LMS '5MT' 4-6-0	44671, 44726, 44756, 44813, 45062, 44886, 45118, 45138, 45435, 45466, 45481
LMS '5XP' 4-6-0	45564, 45579, 45619, 45652, 45704, 45739
BR '5MT' 4-6-0	73069, 73171
'WD' 4-6-0	90763
BR '9F' 2-10-0	92049, 92053, 92151

Locomotives on the depot on 16 May 1961

LMS '3P' 2-6-2T	40193
LMS '2P' 2-6-2T	41273
LMS '5MT' 4-6-0	44659, 44666, 44810, 44944, 45268 *from 21A Saltley* 44673, 44884, 44886, 45334 *from 12A Carlisle Kingmoor.*
LMS '5XP' 4-6-0	45562, 45566, 45577, 45608, 45619, 45658, 45675
'Royal Scot' 4-6-0	46113, 46145
LNER 'A3' 4-6-2	60080, 60092
BR '9F' 2-10-0	92059, 92111

Locomotives on the depot 21 December 1963

BR Class 45/46	D17, D21, D22, D23, D20, D28, D30, D50, D91, D111, D115, D155
BR Class 40	D263
LMS '2P' 2-6-2T	41267 *Stored*
LMS '4P' 2-6-4T	42317
LMS '5MT' 2-6-0	42774, 42812, 42928
LMS '4F' 0-6-0	44400
LMS '5' 4-6-0	44674, 45075, 45324
LMS '5XP' 4-6-0	45564, 45568, 45605, 45639, 45659
LMS '8F' 2-8-0	48116
BR '9F' 2-10-0	92127

Locomotives on the depot 6 February 1966

BR Class 45/46	D13, D70, D112, D167, D173
LNER 'B1' 4-6-0	61327
LNER 'V2' 2-6-2	60887
BR '5MT' 4-6-0	73069
BR '6MT' 4-6-2	72006
BR '7MT' 4-6-2	70008
LMS '5XP' 4-6-0	45562, 45564, 45568, 45573, 45589, 45605, 45608, 45658, 45670

Locomotives present on the last day 2 October 1993. In the morning before leaving

Class 31	31247, 31230, 31563
Class 37	37045, 37059, 37063, 37285
Class 47	47353, 47575, 47566, 47594

Withdrawn:
Class 47: 47433, 47439, 47442, 47448, 47458, 47466, 47515, 47585.

The last locomotive to be fuelled at the depot was Class 37 No 37045.

Back cover:
Rebuilt 'Royal Scot' No 46117 *Welsh Guardsman* is seen at the side of the coaling plant, awaiting its next duty on 4 October 1962, just one month before withdrawal.

Below:
Photographed on 30 September 1993, only two days before the site closed for fuelling and minor repairs, the view from the road bridge presented a sorry sight. There were only two operational locomotives present on roads three and four, the rest are all derelict Class 47s as listed, and as can be seen there was nothing inside the fuelling shed, and so another chapter in the railway history of Leeds closed.